D'Nealian®
Handwriting

2

Author
Donald Neal Thurber

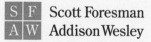

Scott Foresman
Addison Wesley

Editorial Offices: Glenview, Illinois • New York, New York
Sales Offices: Reading, Massachusetts • Atlanta, Georgia
Glenview, Illinois • Carrollton, Texas • Menlo Park, California

1-800-552-2259
http://www.sf.aw.com

Acknowledgments

Text
Page 51: From *The Mother's Day Sandwich.* Text copyright © 1990 by Jillian Wynot. Illustrations copyright © 1990 by Maxie Chambliss. Reprinted with permission of the publisher, Orchard Books, a division of Franklin Watts, Inc.
Page 125: Reprinted with permission of Four Winds Press, an Imprint of Macmillan Publishing Company from *Dinosaurs, Dragonflies & Diamonds: All About Natural History Museums* by Gail Gibbons. Copyright © 1988 by Gail Gibbons.

Illustrations
Laura D'Argo 19, 27, 50, 81, 92; Dawn DeRosa 64, 65, 68, 76, 90, 115, 116, 117, 119; Judith Love 25, 44, 45; Lane Gregory 105, 106, 110; Yoshi Miyake 20, 42, 43; Deborah Morse 100, 101; Jan Palmer 23, 28; Gary Phillips 118; Gail Roth 82; Judy Sakaguchi 58, 75, 89, 111, 123; Jeff Severn 8, 54, 60; Lena Shiffman 30, 31, 32, 33, 34, 35, 37, 39, 40, 97, 98; Georgia Shola 9, 10; Susan Swan 86, 87; Titus Tomescu 18; Jenny Vainsi 67, 94; Joe Veno 69, 91; Darcy Whitehead 3, 4, 5, 11, 29, 49, 59, 84, 85, 93, 102, 103; Jeannie Winston 95

Photographs
Unless otherwise credited, all photographs are the property of Addison Wesley Educational Publishers Inc.
H. Armstrong Roberts, Inc. 72, 73; Photo Researchers/Peter Kaplan 71 (t); Superstock, Inc. 71 (b); Superstock, Inc./M. Roessler (73); Tony Stone Images/Gary Brettnacher 63; Tony Stone Images/Hans Peter Huber 83

Contents

5 Unit One
Getting Ready to Write

6 Left-handed Position for Writing
7 Right-handed Position for Writing
8 Letter Size and Form
9 Letter Slant
10 Letter and Word Spacing

11 Unit Two
Writing Manuscript Letters

12 Writing Manuscript **aA**, **dD**, and **oO**
14 Writing Manuscript **gG** and **cC**
16 Writing Manuscript **eE** and **sS**
18 Practice

19 Review
20 Evaluation
21 Writing Labels
22 Writing Manuscript **fF**, **bB**, and **lL**
24 Writing Manuscript **tT**, **hH**, and **kK**
26 Practice
27 Review
28 Evaluation
29 Writing Directions
30 Writing Manuscript **iI** and **uU**
32 Writing Manuscript **wW** and **yY**
34 Writing Manuscript **jJ** and **rR**
36 Writing Manuscript **nN**, **mM**, and **pP**
38 Practice
39 Review
40 Evaluation
41 Cursive Is Coming
42 Writing Manuscript **qQ** and **vV**
44 Writing Manuscript **zZ** and **xX**
46 Writing Numbers 1 Through 12
48 Practice
49 Review
50 Evaluation
51 Reading and Writing
54 Welcome to the Cursive Club!
55 Strokes That Make Cursive Letters
58 Reading Cursive

59 Unit Three
Writing Lower-case Cursive Letters

60 Letter Size and Form
61 Writing Cursive **l** and **h**
62 Writing Cursive **k** and **t**
63 Writing Cursive **i** and **u**
64 Writing Cursive **e**
65 Writing Cursive **j** and **p**
66 Practice
67 Review
68 Evaluation
69 Writing Cursive **a**
70 Writing Cursive **d** and **c**
71 Writing Cursive **n** and **m**
72 Writing Cursive **x** and **g**
73 Writing Cursive **y** and **q**
74 Practice
75 Review
76 Evaluation
77 Letter Slant and Spacing
78 Writing Cursive **o** and **w**
79 Writing Cursive **b**
80 Practice
81 Review
82 Evaluation
83 Writing Cursive **v** and **z**
84 Writing Cursive **s**
85 Writing Cursive **r**
86 Writing Cursive **f**
87 Joining Sidestroke Letters
88 Practice
89 Review
90 Evaluation
91 Letter Size, Form, Slant, and Spacing
92 Writing a List

93 Unit Four
Writing Capital Cursive Letters

94 Writing Cursive **A** and **C**
95 Writing Cursive **E** and **O**
96 Practice
97 Review
98 Evaluation
99 Addressing an Envelope
100 Writing Cursive **H** and **K**
101 Writing Cursive **N** and **M**
102 Writing Cursive **U** and **V**
103 Writing Cursive **W** and **Y**
104 Practice
105 Review
106 Evaluation
107 Writing Proper Nouns
108 Writing Cursive **T** and **F**
109 Writing Cursive **B**
110 Writing Cursive **P** and **R**
111 Writing an Invitation
112 Practice
113 Review
114 Evaluation
115 Writing Cursive **G** and **S**
116 Writing Cursive **I**
117 Writing Cursive **Q** and **Z**
118 Writing Cursive **D**
119 Writing Cursive **J**
120 Writing Cursive **X** and **L**
121 Writing a Thank-you Note
122 Practice
123 Review
124 Evaluation
125 Reading and Writing
128 Index

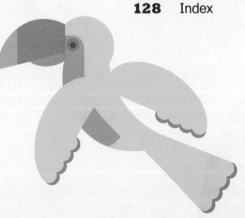

Unit One

Getting Ready to Write

Left-handed Position for Writing

Sit tall.
Put both feet on the floor.

Slant your paper as shown in the picture.
Hold it with your right hand.

Hold your pencil lightly between
your fingers. Study the picture.

Right-handed Position for Writing

Sit tall. Put both feet on the floor.

Slant your paper as shown in the picture. Hold it with your left hand.

Hold your pencil lightly between your fingers. Study the picture.

Letter Size and Form

a c e i m n o r s u v w x z

b d f h k l t   g j p q y

Manuscript letters have only three sizes. There are small letters, tall letters, and letters with descenders.

Small letters sit on the bottom line. They touch the middle line. Write three small letters.

Tall letters also sit on the bottom line. They touch the top line. Write three tall letters.

Descend means "go down." Letters with descenders have tails that go down under the bottom line. The descenders touch the line below. Write three letters with descenders.

Forming letters correctly helps make handwriting easy to read. Some letters, like **a** and **b,** must be closed. The letters **t** and **f** must be crossed. Dot the letters **i** and **j.**

Can you read the word below?

gift

The word is **gift.** Why is it so hard to read? What did the writer forget to do?

Write the word **gift** correctly. Close the letter **g.** Dot the **i.** Cross the **f** and the **t.**

Is your word easier to read?

Letter Slant

Slant all your letters the same way. That will make your handwriting easier to read.

Some writers slant their letters to the right.

right

Some writers slant their letters to the left.

left

Some writers make their letters straight up and down.

up and down

Do not slant letters different ways.

different

Write **Slant letters one way.**

Which way do your letters slant?

Do they all slant the same way?   Yes ☐   No ☐

Letter and Word Spacing

Correct spacing makes handwriting easier to read. When you write a word, be sure the letters are evenly spaced.

Don't write letters in a word too close together.

Don't write letters in a word too far apart. They won't look as if they are part of the word.

fish

f i s h

Words in a sentence also have to be spaced correctly. Leave more space between words than between letters in a word. That way each word stands out. Trace this sentence. It has correct spacing.

The fish can swim.

Here is a sentence that is not spaced correctly. Do you know what it says? Write the sentence with correct spacing.

Canyoureadthis?

Is your sentence easier to read?   Yes ☐   No ☐

Unit Two

Writing Manuscript Letters

Writing Manuscript aA, dD, and oO

Trace and write the letters.

a

A

d

D

o

O

Trace and write the names.
Remember that names begin with capital letters.

Adam

Adam

Donna

Donna

Olivia

Olivia

Trace and write the sentences.
Sentences begin with captial letters too.
A sentence that is a statement ends with a period. [.]

Anna loves dinosaurs.

Anna loves dinosaurs.

A sentence that is a question ends with a
question mark. [?]

Does Owen make models?

Does Owen make models?

Writing Manuscript gG and Cc

Trace and write the letters.

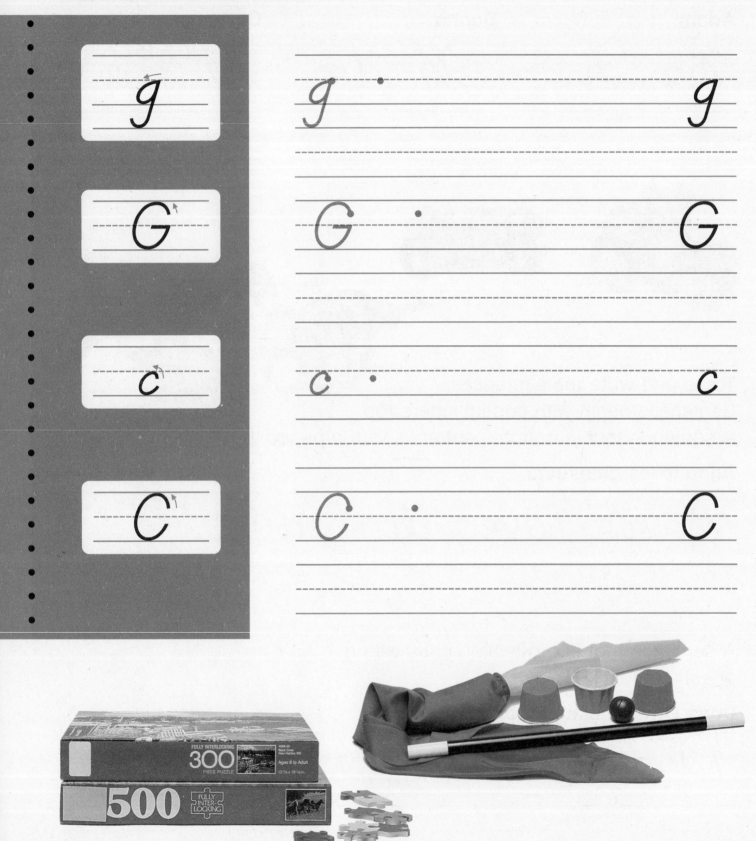

Trace and write the names.

Grace

Grace

Craig

Craig

Casey

Casey

Trace and write the sentences.

Gail collects rocks.

Gail collects rocks.

Glen can do big puzzles.

Glen can do big puzzles.

Can Cal do magic tricks?

Can Cal do magic tricks?

15

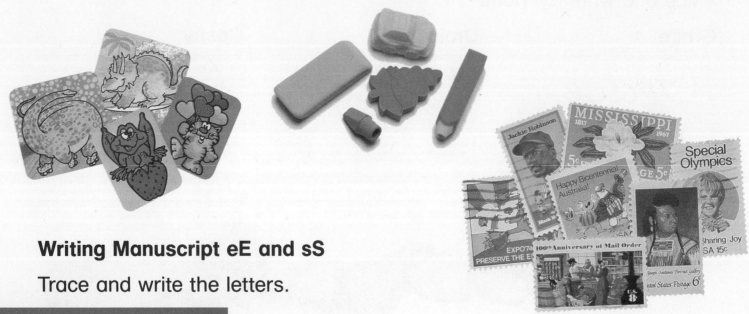

Writing Manuscript eE and sS

Trace and write the letters.

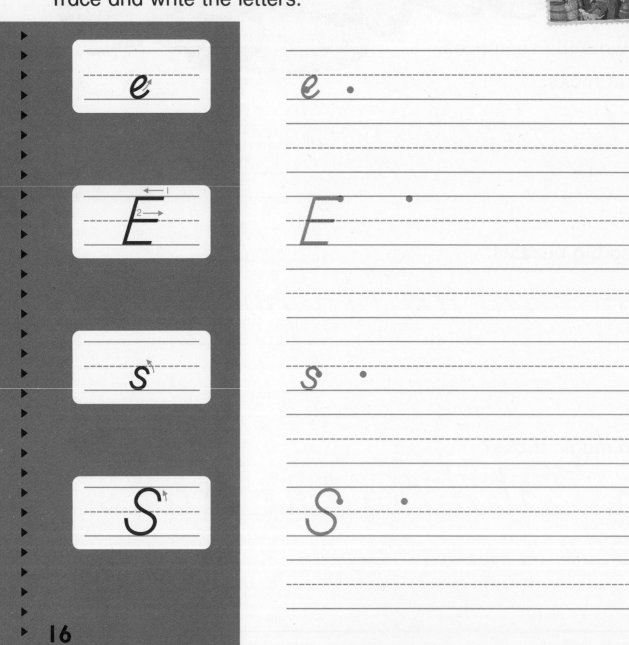

e ·   e

E ·   E

s ·   s

S ·   S

Trace and write the names.

Steve

Steve

Elise

Elise

Sue

Sue

Trace and write the sentences.

Erin likes stickers.

Erin likes stickers.

Scott has erasers.

Scott has erasers.

Ellen saves stamps.

Ellen saves stamps.

Practice

Write the letters.

a   a

d   d

o   o

g   g

c   c

e   e

s   s

A   D

O   G

C   E   S

Circle your best letter in each line.

18

ⓐ

Review

Write the words and names.

leaves

coins

Carol

award

caps

Gregory

baseball cards

Evaluation

Write the sentences.

One coin is from Spain.

Each stamp is special.

Alex and Donald got an award.

Check Your Handwriting
Are your **a**, **d**, **o**, and **g** closed?

Yes ☐   No ☐

Writing Labels

Dawn and her family went to Michigan for their vacation. Dawn collected some special things from her trip. She arranged her collection in a box. She put a label next to each thing in the box.

Fill in the labels for Dawn's collection. Write smaller than usual to fit the words on the labels. Use the words at the right.

special stones
shells
wooden shoes
postcards
old money
patch

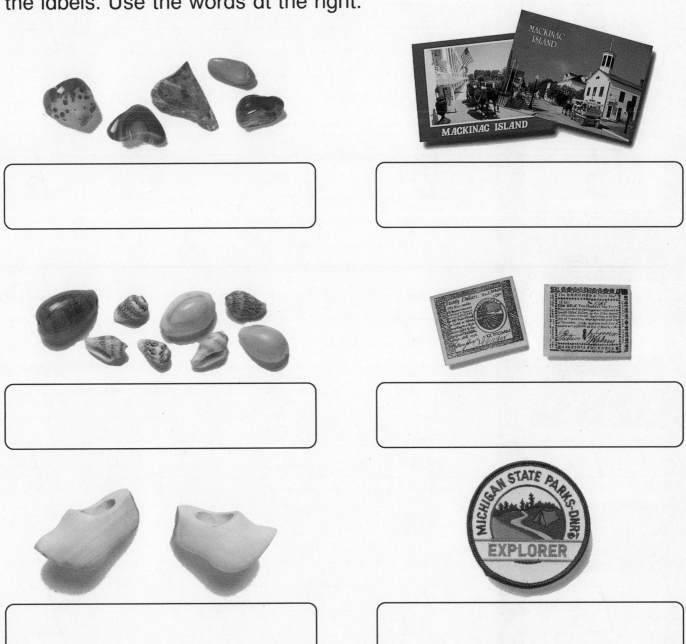

Writing Manuscript fF, bB, and lL

Trace and write the letters.

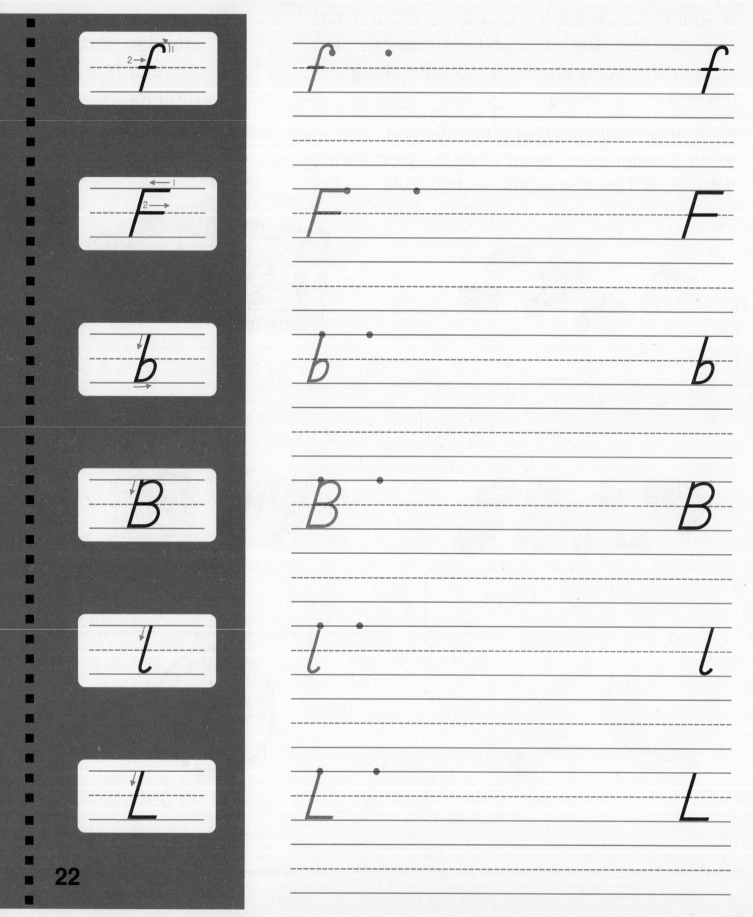

Trace and write the sentences.
Remember the apostrophes. [']
A sentence that shows strong feeling
ends with an exclamation mark. [!]

Let's be careful!

Let's be careful!

Follow traffic signals.

Follow traffic signals.

Barb's bicycle has a bell and a flag.

Barb's bicycle has a bell and a flag.

Writing Manuscript tT, hH, and kK

Trace and write the letters.

t   t

T   T

h   h

H   H

k   k

K   K

Trace and write the sentences.
Remember the comma. [,]

Keep to the right.

Keep to the right.

Helmets help keep bike riders safe.

Helmets help keep bike riders safe.

Turn left here, Keith.

Turn left here, Keith.

Practice

Write the letters.

f   f

b   b

l   l

t   t

h   h

k   k

F   F   T   T

B   B   H   H

L   L   K   K

Circle your best letter in each line.

f

Review

Write the words and names.

bike

flag

helmet

basket

Frank

Beth

traffic light

Evaluation

Remember: Tall letters should touch the top line.

Write the sentences.

The bike got a flat tire.

_____

- -

_____

_____

Hal has a tire patch kit.

_____

- -

_____

_____

Libby and Kirk follow the bike path.

_____

- -

_____

_____

_____

Check Your Handwriting
Do your tall letters touch the top line?

Yes No
☐   ☐

28

Writing Directions

Taylor will ride his bike to his friend Leon's house after school. Leon gave Taylor directions. Leon's directions are neatly written. Taylor can read them easily.

Copy Leon's directions. Make sure your letters are evenly spaced. Leave more space between words than between letters in a word.

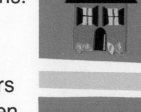

Bell Lane

King School

Fifth Street

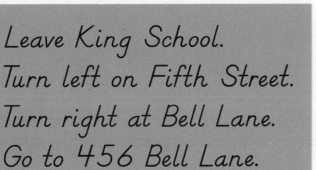

Leave King School.
Turn left on Fifth Street.
Turn right at Bell Lane.
Go to 456 Bell Lane.

Writing Manuscript iI and uU

Trace and write the letters.

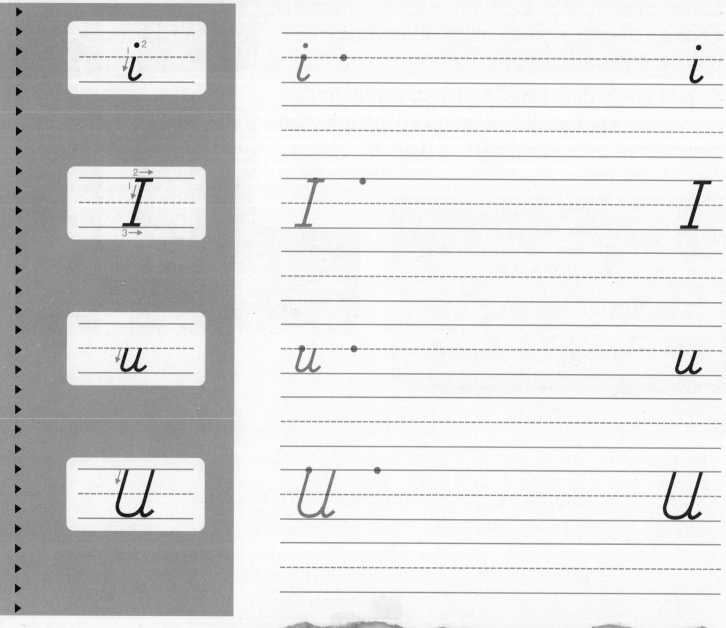

Trace and write the sentences.
Remember that the pronoun **I** is always capitalized.

I will play a unicorn.

I will play a unicorn.

Invite your family and your friends.

Invite your family and your friends.

Up goes the curtain!

Up goes the curtain!

Writing Manuscript wW and yY

Trace and write the letters.

w   w

W   W

y   y

Y   Y

Trace and write the sentences.

We worked on Wednesday.

We worked on Wednesday.

Wendy drew a yellow sun.

Wendy drew a yellow sun.

Yoshi drew windows.

Yoshi drew windows.

We were very busy.

We were very busy.

Writing Manuscript jJ and rR

Trace and write the letters.

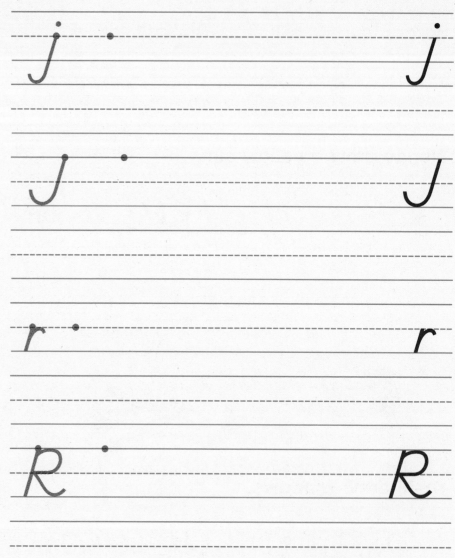

j   j

J   J

r   r

R   R

Talent Show

Trace and write the names.

Jordan

Robyn

Jordan

Robyn

Trace and write the sentences.

Jerry tells great jokes.

Jerry tells great jokes.

Rosa juggles red balls.

Rosa juggles red balls.

Juggling is hard!

Juggling is hard!

Writing Manuscript nN, mM, and pP

Trace and write the letters.

n   n

N   N

m   m

M   M

p   p

P   P

Trace and write the sentences.

Nick made nine nice animal masks.

Nick made nine nice animal masks.

Pam practiced her part.

Pam practiced her part.

Mindy needs makeup.

Mindy needs makeup.

37

Practice

Write the letters.

i	i	I	I
u	u	U	U
w	w	W	W
y	y	Y	Y
j	j	J	J
r	r	R	R
n	n	N	N
m	m	M	M
p	p	P	P

Circle your best letter in each line.

38

Review

Write the words and names.

makeup
_____

_____

unicorn
_____

_____

William
_____

_____

Prince Jim's crown
_____

_____

jewelry
_____

_____

Nancy
_____

_____

Ursula
_____

_____

Evaluation

 **Remember:** Slant all letters the same way.

Write the sentences.

Mary and Ian perform.

_____

- - - - - - - - - - - - - - - - - - -

_____

Ryan wears a costume.

_____

- - - - - - - - - - - - - - - - - - -

_____

You will enjoy our program.

_____

- - - - - - - - - - - - - - - - - - -

_____

_____

- - - - - - - - - - - - - - - - - - -

_____

 **Check Your Handwriting**   Yes   No
Do all your letters slant the same way?   ☐   ☐

Cursive Is Coming

Sarah's class makes lists of what is served in the school lunchroom every day.

Sarah and her teacher wrote their lists in different ways. Most of the letters are joined in Mrs. Stone's list.

One place where letters are joined has been marked for you. Mark two more places where letters are joined.

Manuscript
You already know how to write like this.

Cursive
You will soon learn how to write like this.

Lunchroom Menu	Lunchroom Menu
Name *Sarah*	Name *Mrs. Stone*
Day *Friday*	Day *Friday*
pizza	*pizza*
salad	*salad*
fruit cup	*fruit cup*
milk	*milk*

Writing Manuscript qQ and vV

Trace and write the letters.

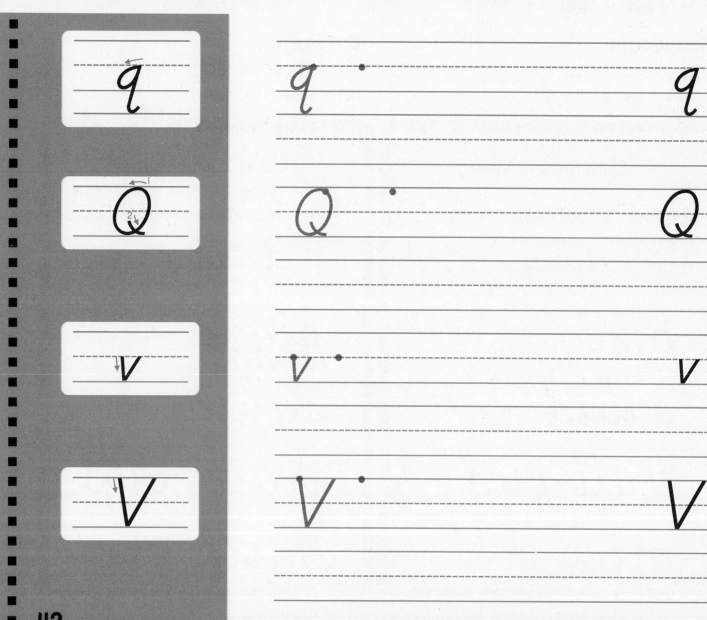

Trace and write the sentences.

Quinn bought seven quarts of milk.

Quinn bought seven quarts of milk.

Vic is quite lucky to have five quarters.

Vic is quite lucky to have five quarters.

Vi shops very quickly.

Vi shops very quickly.

43

Writing Manuscript zZ and xX

Trace and write the letters.

z

Z

x

X

Trace and write the sentences.
Remember that the title **Mrs.** begins with
a capital letter and ends with a period.

**Mrs. Xavier got an extra box of cereal
and some pancake mix.**

Mrs. Xavier got an extra

box of cereal and some

pancake mix.

Zoe needs six frozen pizzas.

Zoe needs six frozen

pizzas.

Writing Numbers 1 Through 12

Trace and write the numbers.

1   1   1

2   2   2

3   3   3

4   4   4

5   5   5

6   6   6

7   7   7

8   8   8

9   9   9

10   10   10

11   11   11

12   12   12

Trace and write the number words.

one

one

two

two

three

three

four

four

five

five

six

six

seven

seven

eight

eight

nine

nine

ten

ten

eleven

eleven

twelve

twelve

Practice

Write the letters.

q   q   Q   Q

V   V   V   V

z   z   Z   Z

x   x   X   X

Write the numbers.

1   1   7   7

2   2   8   8

3   3   9   9

4   4   10   10

5   5   11   11

6   6   12   12

Circle your best letter or number in each line.

Review

Write the words.

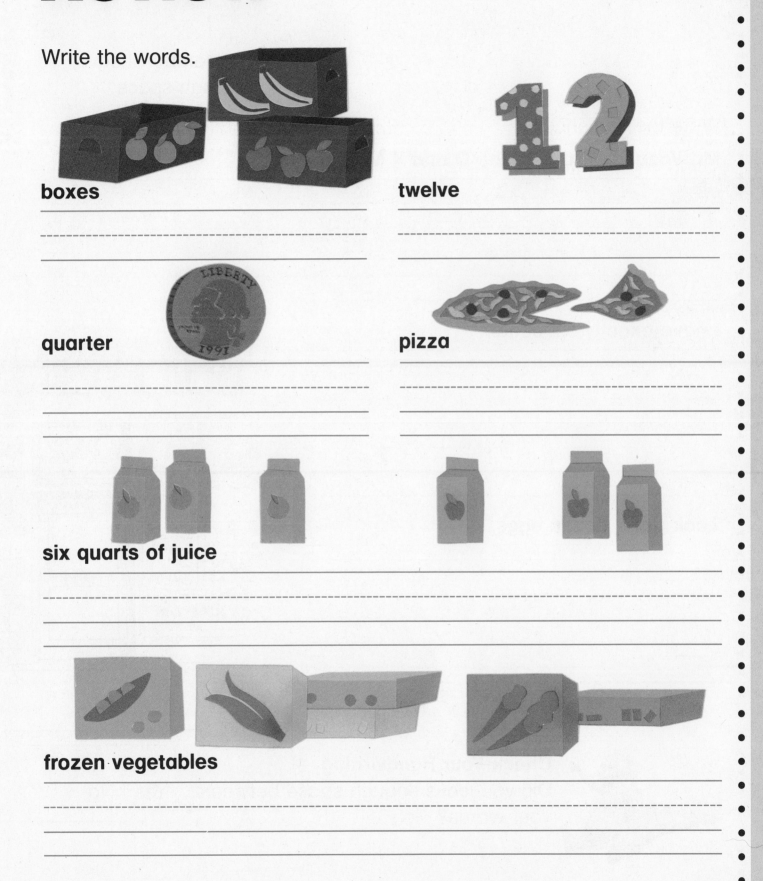

boxes

_____

- - - - - - - - - - - - - - -

_____

twelve

- - - - - - - - - - - - - - -

_____

quarter

- - - - - - - - - - - - - - -

_____

pizza

- - - - - - - - - - - - - - -

_____

six quarts of juice

- - - - - - - - - - - - - - -

_____

_____

frozen vegetables

_____

- - - - - - - - - - - - - - -

_____

Evaluation

Remember: Leave enough space between words.

Write the sentences.

Mr. Vazquez drove to the Q and X Market.

_____

- -

_____

_____

_____

I have exactly six cents.

_____

_____

- -

_____

_____

Zack got a dozen eggs.

- -

_____

_____

- -

_____

Check Your Handwriting
Did you leave enough space between your words?

Yes No
☐   ☐

Reading and Writing

In the book *The Mother's Day Sandwich* by Jillian Wynot, Hackett and Ivy made a surprise breakfast for their mother. All the food spilled and their surprise flopped.

Read this part of the story to find out what Mama did to make Hackett and Ivy feel better.

Mama pulled them back. "You don't make a Mother's Day sandwich in the kitchen. You can make it right here."

"Here?" said Ivy.

"Yes," said Mama. "You be one slice of bread, Ivy. And Hackett, you be the other slice. And I will be the cheese."

Hackett and Ivy giggled.

"Now, listen, you two pieces of bread," said Mama. "Squeeze very close to the cheese, so it can't fall out."

Ivy and Hackett squeezed very close to the cheese.

"Happy Mother's Day," said the two slices of bread.

"Thank you," said the cheese.

Think about a surprise sandwich you might make for someone special. Write some words in the Word Bank below to help you tell about this sandwich.

Word Bank

_____   _____
- - - - - - - - - - - - - - - -   - - - - - - - - - - - - - - - -
_____   _____
- - - - - - - - - - - - - - - -   - - - - - - - - - - - - - - - -
_____   _____
- - - - - - - - - - - - - - - -   - - - - - - - - - - - - - - - -

Kristin decided to write about a surprise sandwich.
Read the sentence she wrote to start her story.

I would make a pretty sandwich of tiny stars cut out of baloney.

Look at what Kristin wrote.   Yes   No
- Did she use describing words to tell about
  her surprise sandwich?   ☐   ☐
- Can you picture the sandwich Kristin would make?   ☐   ☐

Look at how Kristin wrote it.
- Do all her small letters touch the middle line?   ☐   ☐
- Do all her tall letters touch the top line?   ☐   ☐
- Do all her descenders touch the line below?   ☐   ☐

Circle any letters that are not the correct size.

52

Now it's your turn to write. Describe a surprise
sandwich you might make for someone special. You
may want to use the words from your Word Bank.

Look at what you wrote.

	Yes	No
• Did you use any describing words to tell about your surprise sandwich?	☐	☐
• Would a person reading about your sandwich be able to picture it?	☐	☐

Look at how you wrote it.

• Do your small letters touch the middle line?	☐	☐
• Do your tall letters touch the top line?	☐	☐
• Do your descenders touch the line below?	☐	☐

Make any changes that are needed. Then
make a clean copy on another sheet of paper.

Welcome to the
Cursive Club!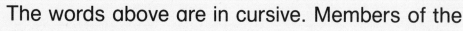

The words above are in cursive. Members of the Cursive Club can read and write in cursive. What does cursive look like to you?

cooked spaghetti?	a secret code?	letters you already know?
	∵ ⠿ — ∠ ○ ⅃ ∧△ ·· ∟ ∞ ⊡ ∠∠ — ∷	*Do you know cursive?*

You're right if you said cursive looks like letters you already know. Look at each letter in the messages below. Circle the cursive letters that look almost the same as manuscript letters.

We can't wait for cursive!

We can't wait for cursive!

Most cursive letters are joined together. Make a ⌣ under five places where letters are joined.

Congratulations! You are learning cursive. Soon you will be a member of the Cursive Club!

Strokes That Make Cursive Letters

To write cursive **l, h, k, t, i, u,** and **e,** add **uphill strokes** to the letters you already know. These letters already have ending strokes. To write cursive **j** and **p,** begin with an uphill stroke and add an ending stroke.

uphill strokes

With your finger, trace the red uphill stroke in each letter. Circle the ending stroke in each letter.

l h k t i u e   j p

Uphill strokes can be tall or short. Practice each one.

To write a word in cursive, join the ending stroke in one letter with the beginning stroke in the next letter.

The letters **k, i, t,** and **e** begin with uphill strokes. Ending strokes and uphill strokes are joined in the word **kite.** Trace the word.

kite   kite

55

To write cursive **a, d, c, n, m,** and **x,** add **overhill strokes** to the letters you already know. These letters already have ending strokes. To write cursive **g, y,** and **q,** begin with an overhill stroke and add an ending stroke.

With your finger, trace the red overhill stroke in each letter. Circle the ending stroke in each letter.

overhill stroke

a d c n m x   g y q

Practice the overhill stroke.

The letters **m, a, n,** and **y** begin with overhill strokes. Ending strokes and overhill strokes are joined in the word **many.** Trace the word.

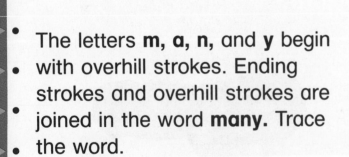

m a n y   many

The cursive letters **o, w,** and **b** end with a **sidestroke.**

With your finger, trace the red sidestroke in each letter.

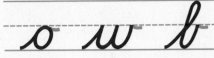

Practice the sidestroke.

sidestroke

A letter with a sidestroke must join the following letter near the middle line. This changes the beginning stroke of the following letter. Notice how the sidestroke changes **n, y,** and **e** in the words below. Trace the words.

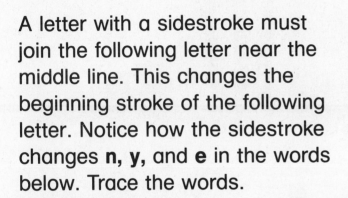

Most cursive letters look like the manuscript letters you already know. The letters **v, z, s, r,** and **f** look different.

Circle the uphill letters. Underline the overhill letters. Put a ✔ above the sidestroke letter.

v v   z z   s s   r r   f f

Reading Cursive

Three messages are in the Cursive Clubhouse.
The writer has torn the messages in half.
Draw a line from the beginning of each
message to its missing part.

The party

a friend.

It's at the

is today.

Bring

clubhouse.

Unit Three

Writing Lower-case Cursive Letters

Letter Size and Form

Cursive letters come in the same three sizes as manuscript letters. There are small letters, tall letters, and letters with descenders.

Trace these small letters.

Trace these tall letters.

Trace these letters with descenders.

You want people to be able to read what you have written. To make your handwriting easy to read, be sure to form your letters correctly. Here are some things to remember about forming cursive letters.

Some cursive letters must be closed.

Some cursive letters have loops.

You must retrace when you write some cursive letters.

Look at the cursive alphabet below. Circle four letters that must be closed. Underline five letters that have loops. Put a ✓ above three letters that have retracing.

a b c d e f g h i j

k l m n o p q r

s t u v w x y z

Writing Cursive l and h

You can see manuscript **l** and **h** in cursive
l and **h.** Begin with an uphill stroke.
Trace and write the letters.

l l   *l   l   .   .   .   l*

h h   *h   h   .   .   .   h*

Most cursive letters are joined near the
bottom line. Practice joining these letters.

ll ll   *ll*

hh hh   *hh*

lh lh   *lh*

hl hl   *hl*

Writing Cursive k and t

You can see manuscript **k** and **t** in cursive
k and **t**. Begin with an uphill stroke.
Trace and write the letters.

k   k   k   .   .   .   k

t   t   t   .   .   .   t

Remember that most cursive letters are joined
near the bottom line. Join the letters.

kl   kl   kl

th   th   th

lk   lk   lk

ht   ht   ht

tl   tl   tl

Writing Cursive i and u

You can see manuscript **i** and **u** in cursive
i and **u.** Begin with an uphill stroke.
Trace and write the letters.

Now you can join letters in words.
Trace and write the words.

hill

hill

it

it

kit

kit

hut

hut

lit

lit

Writing Cursive e

You can see manuscript **e** in cursive **e.**
Begin with an uphill stroke.
Trace and write the letter.

e e

e e e .   .   . e

Trace and write the words.

hike

hike

tell

tell

he

he

tie

tie

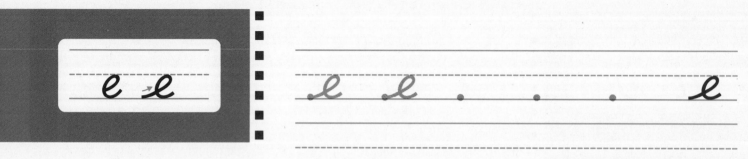

the little kettle

the little kettle

Writing Cursive j and p

You can see manuscript **j** and **p** in cursive **j** and **p.** Begin with an uphill stroke. Add an ending stroke. Trace and write the letters.

Trace and write the words.

jeep

jeep

help

help

peek

peek

help put up

help put up

Practice

Write the letters.

l   l

h   h

k   k

t   t

i   i

u   u

e   e

j   j

p   p

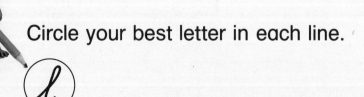

Circle your best letter in each line.

l

Review

Write the words.

kit

_____
- - - - - - - - - - - - - - - -
_____

kettle

_____
- - - - - - - - - - - - - - - -
_____

hut

_____
- - - - - - - - - - - - - - - -
_____

pup

_____
- - - - - - - - - - - - - - - -
_____

elk

_____
- - - - - - - - - - - - - - - -
_____

jeep

_____
- - - - - - - - - - - - - - - -
_____

heel

_____
- - - - - - - - - - - - - - - -
_____

hill

_____
- - - - - - - - - - - - - - - -
_____

Evaluation

Remember: Cross the letter **t** and dot the letters **i** and **j**.

Write the words.

kept the jeep

the little kettle

the hike up the hill

Check Your Handwriting

	Yes	No
Did you cross the letter **t**?	☐	☐
Did you dot the letters **i** and **j**?	☐	☐

Writing Cursive a

You can see manuscript **a** in cursive **a**.
Begin with an overhill stroke.
Trace and write the letter.

a a a   *a a a . . . a*

Remember that most cursive letters
are joined near the bottom line.
Trace and write the words.

ape

ape

apple

apple

eat

eat

ate that apple

ate that apple

Writing Cursive d and c

You can see manuscript **d** and **c** in cursive **d** and **c**. Begin with an overhill stroke. Trace and write the letters.

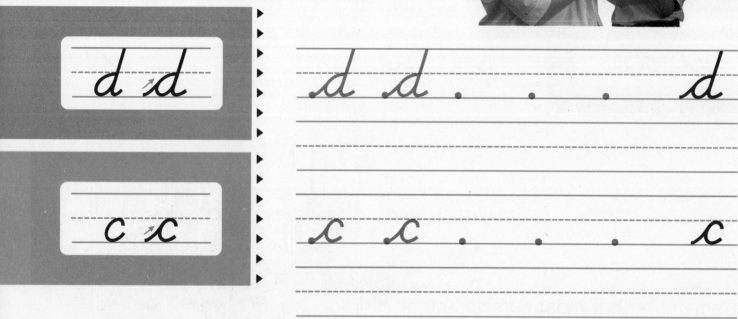

Trace and write the words.

duck

duck

child

child

chick

chick

held the duck

held the duck

Writing Cursive n and m

You can see manuscript **n** and **m** in cursive **n** and **m.** Begin with an overhill stroke. Trace and write the letters.

n n

m m

n n n . . n

m m m . . m

Trace and write the words.

an animal

an animal

a llama and a camel

a llama and a camel

Writing Cursive x and g

You can see manuscript **x** and **g** in cursive **x** and **g.** Begin with an overhill stroke. Add an ending stroke to **g.** Trace and write the letters.

x   x

x   x   .   .   .   x

g   g

g   g   .   .   .   g

Trace and write the words.

king

king

jungle

jungle

huge

huge

in the next cage

in the next cage

72

Writing Cursive y and q

You can see manuscript **y** and **q** in cursive
y and **q.** Begin with an overhill stroke. Add an
ending stroke. Trace and write the letters.

y y   *y   y   .   .   .   y*

q q   *q   q   .   .   .   q*

Trace and write the words.

quite tiny

quite tiny

play quietly

play quietly

Practice

Write the letters.

a   *a*

d   *d*

c   *c*

n   *n*

m   *m*

x   *x*

g   *g*

y   *y*

q   *q*

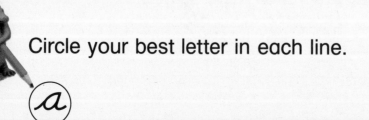

Circle your best letter in each line.

Review

Write the words.

panda

cage

exit

penguin

a quick chimp

a chilly animal

Evaluation

Remember: The letters **g, y,** and **q** have descenders. The descenders should touch the line below.

Write the words.

a huge mane

a quacking duck

my exciting day

Check Your Handwriting
Do your descenders touch the line below?

Yes No
☐   ☐

Letter Slant and Spacing

When you write in cursive, slant all your letters the same way. You may slant your letters to the right or to the left. You may write them straight up and down. Do not slant your letters in different ways.

right   *left*

up and down   *different*

Which writing is hard to read? Why is it hard?

Use correct spacing when you write. The letters in a word should be evenly spaced. Leave more space between words than between letters in a word.

ahugecat   *a huge cat*

Which writing is easier to read? Why is it easier?

Write these words. Slant all your letters the same way. Use correct spacing.

hidden in the jungle

	Yes	No
Do all your letters slant the same way?	☐	☐
Are the letters in your words evenly spaced?	☐	☐
Did you leave enough space between the words?	☐	☐

Writing Cursive o and w

You can see manuscript **o** and **w** in cursive **o** and **w.** Begin cursive **o** with an overhill stroke. Begin cursive **w** with an uphill stroke. Both letters end with a sidestroke. Trace and write the letters.

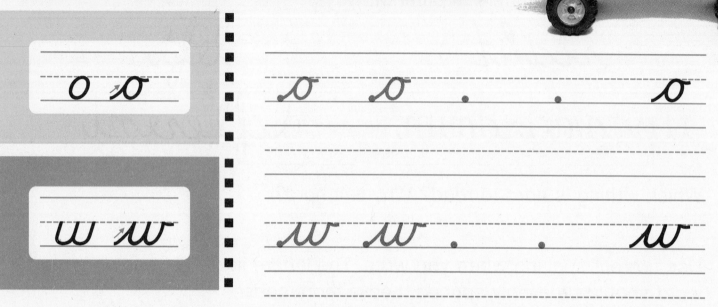

Cursive **o** and **w** join the next letter near the middle line. This changes the beginning stroke of the next letter. Trace and write the words.

a yellow yoyo

a yellow yoyo

a new wagon

a new wagon

Writing Cursive b

Cursive **b** looks a little like manuscript **b**. Begin with an uphill stroke and end with a sidestroke. Trace and write the letter.

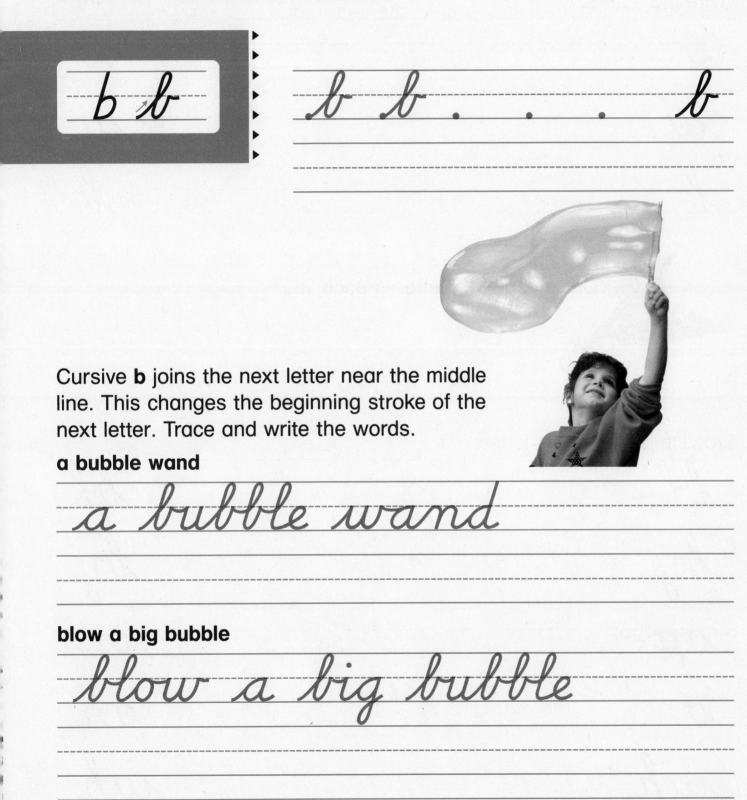

b b

b b . . . b

Cursive **b** joins the next letter near the middle line. This changes the beginning stroke of the next letter. Trace and write the words.

a bubble wand

a bubble wand

blow a big bubble

blow a big bubble

Practice

Write the letters.

o   o

w   w

b   b

Circle your best letter in each line.

Practice joining these letters.

bl   bl

by   by

op   op

on   on

wh   wh

Review

Write the words.

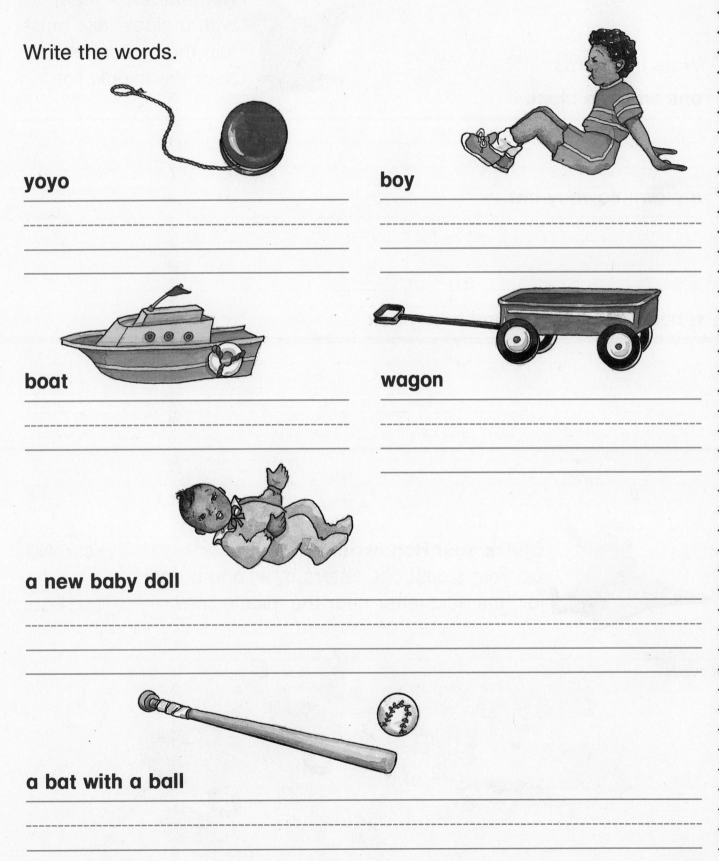

yoyo

boy

boat

wagon

a new baby doll

a bat with a ball

Evaluation

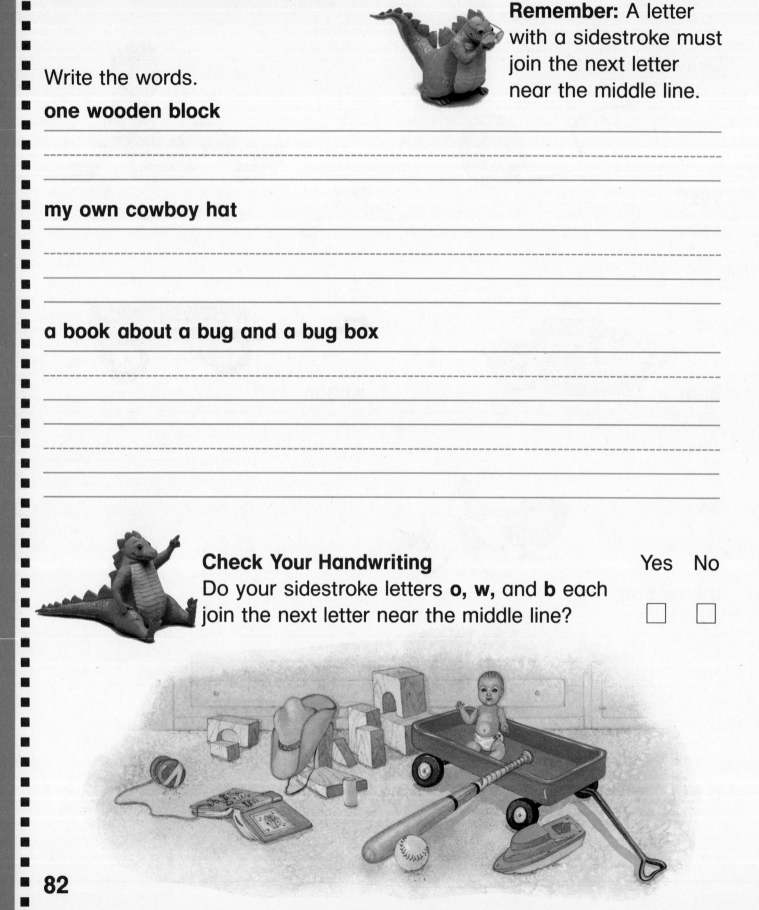

Remember: A letter with a sidestroke must join the next letter near the middle line.

Write the words.

one wooden block

_____
- -
_____

my own cowboy hat

_____
- -
_____

a book about a bug and a bug box

_____
- -
_____
_____

Check Your Handwriting
Do your sidestroke letters **o, w,** and **b** each join the next letter near the middle line?

	Yes	No
	☐	☐

Writing Cursive v and z

Cursive **v** and **z** do not look like manuscript **v** and **z**. Begin cursive **v** and **z** with an overhill stroke. Cursive **v** ends with a sidestroke. Trace and write the letters.

Trace and write the words.

a lazy day

a lazy day

a lovely view

a lovely view

83

Writing Cursive s

Cursive **s** does not look like manuscript **s.**
Begin cursive **s** with an uphill stroke. Trace
and write the letter.

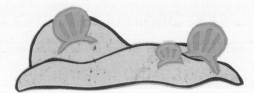

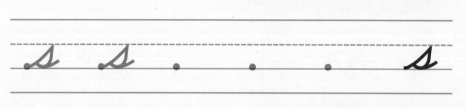

Trace and write the words.

sandy

sandy

sunny

sunny

sea and sand

sea and sand

shells on castles

shells on castles

Writing Cursive r

Cursive **r** does not look like manuscript **r**. Begin cursive **r** with an uphill stroke. Trace and write the letter.

r r

r r . . . r

Trace and write the words.

under the water

under the water

three large crabs in a hurry

three large crabs in a hurry

Writing Cursive f

Cursive **f** does not look like manuscript **f**.
Begin cursive **f** with an uphill stroke. Trace
and write the letter.

Trace and write the words.

fancy fins on fish

fancy fins on fish

five different fish

five different fish

Joining Sidestroke Letters

The letters **o, w, b,** and **v** must join the next letter near the middle line. This changes the beginning stroke of the next letter. Trace and write the joined letters and words.

ve ve ve

dive

br br br

brave

or or or

shore

os os os

toss

ws ws ws

claws

Practice

Write the letters.

v v

z z

s s

r r

f f

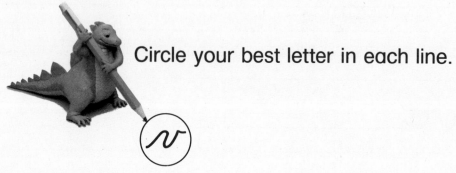

Circle your best letter in each line.

Practice joining these letters.

fr shr

vy zz

Review

Write the words.

shovel

waves

starfish

shark

a dozen shells

very fluffy towels

Evaluation

Remember: Small letters should touch the middle line.

Write the words.

your first dive

fish zooming past

my favorite seashell

Check Your Handwriting
Do your small letters touch the middle line?

Yes ☐ No ☐

Letter Size, Form, Slant, and Spacing

Write the words in your best cursive handwriting.

Form your letters correctly.

as red as a lobster

Did you form your letters correctly?   Yes ☐   No ☐

Make your letters the right height.

as slippery as an eel

Did you make your letters the right height?   Yes ☐   No ☐

Slant all your letters the same way.

like a fish out of water

Did you slant all your letters the same way?   Yes ☐   No ☐

Use correct letter and word spacing.

as happy as a clam

Did you use correct letter and word spacing?   Yes ☐   No ☐

Writing a List

The Parks family planned a trip to the beach. Mrs. Parks made a list of things to bring. Copy her list on the lines below. Plan your writing so that each thing on the list fits on one line.

two old blankets
five towels
a beach umbrella
sunscreen
pails and shovels
juice and popcorn
cups and napkins

Unit Four

Writing Capital Cursive Letters

Writing Cursive A and C

Cursive **A** does not look like manuscript **A**.
Cursive **C** looks like manuscript **C**.
Trace and write the letters.

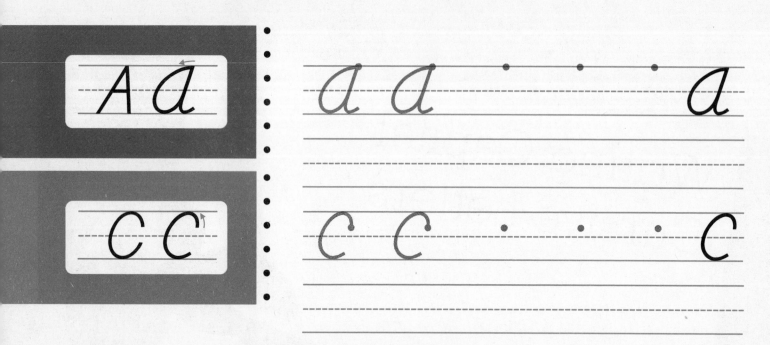

Trace and write the sentence. Be sure to join
cursive **A** and **C** to the letter that comes next.

Come to the amazing Apollo Circus!

Come to the amazing

Apollo Circus!

Writing Cursive E and O

Cursive **E** looks a little like manuscript **E**.
You can see manuscript **O** in cursive **O**.
Trace and write the letters.

Trace and write the sentences.
Join cursive **E** to the letter that follows it.
Do not join cursive **O** to the next letter.

Elephants take a bow.

Elephants take a bow.

Omar trains them.

Omar trains them.

Practice

Write the letters.

a   *a*

C   *C*

E   *E*

O   *O*

Circle your best letter in each line.

Write the names.

Ollie's Clown Company

Eva's Acrobats

Annie's Animals

Review

Write the words and sentences from the signs. Use cursive.

Entrance

_____
_____
_____

Exit

_____
_____
_____

The Omni Circus
Come One! Come All!

"Enjoy Amazing Acts from
Around the Country"

Otto

_____
_____
_____

Ajax

_____
_____
_____

Come One! Come All!

_____
_____
_____

Evaluation

Remember: Capital **A**, **C**, and **E** should be joined to the letters that follow them.

Write the sentences.

Everyone enjoys Elmo.

_____
- -
_____
_____

Coco the clown went to Clown College.

_____
- -
_____
_____
- -
_____
_____

Once Al saw a circus.

_____
- -
_____
_____

Check Your Handwriting   Yes   No
Do your capital **A**, **C**, and **E**
join the letters that follow them?   ☐   ☐

Addressing an Envelope

Carla wrote to her pen pal, Andrew, to tell him about the circus. Then she addressed an envelope for her letter.

Copy the addresses in the space below. Form your letters and numbers correctly so the Postal Service will know where to deliver the letter. Try to keep your writing straight even though there are no writing lines. Notice that the addresses are written in capital manuscript letters.

CARLA CRUZ
605 ELM AVENUE
OAKLAND CA 94610

ANDREW EVANS
77 OAK COURT
ORLANDO FL 32804

Writing Cursive H and K

You can see manuscript **H** and **K** in cursive **H** and **K**. Trace and write the letters.

Trace and write the sentence.
Join cursive **K** to the letter that follows it.
Do not join cursive **H** to the next letter.

Kathy Hobbs works at Kane Hospital.

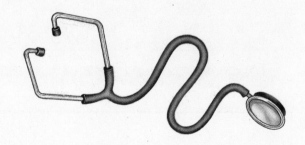

Kathy Hobbs works at Kane Hospital.

Writing Cursive N and M

Cursive **N** and **M** look a little like manuscript
N and **M**. Trace and write the letters.

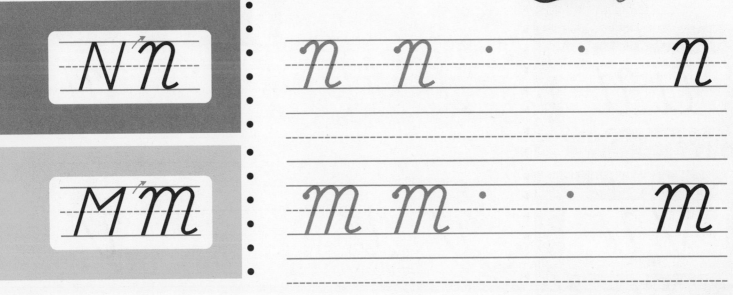

Trace and write the sentence. Join cursive **N**
and **M** to the letters that follow them.

Mr. Nash plays in the Melody Makers.

*Mr. Nash plays in the
Melody Makers.*

Writing Cursive U and V

Cursive **U** looks very much like manuscript **U**.
Cursive **V** looks a little like manuscript **V**.
Trace and write the letters.

Trace and write the sentence.
Join cursive **U** to the letter that follows it.
Do not join cursive **V** to the next letter.

Uncle Vic is a waiter at the Village Cafe.

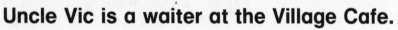

Uncle Vic is a waiter at the Village Cafe.

Writing Cursive W and Y

Cursive **W** and **Y** look a little like manuscript **W** and **Y**. Trace and write the letters.

W   W   W

Y   Y   Y

Trace and write the sentence.
Join cursive **Y** to the letter that follows it.
Do not join cursive **W** to the next letter.

Yes, Yolanda works for World Airlines.

Yes, Yolanda works for
World Airlines.

Practice

Write the letters.

$\mathcal{H}$ $\mathcal{H}$

$\mathcal{K}$ $\mathcal{K}$

n n

m m

u u

v v

w w

y y

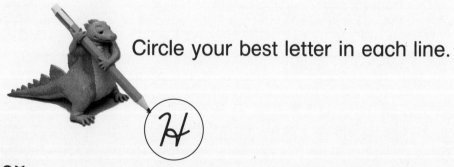

Circle your best letter in each line.

104

Review

Mr. Chandler's class wrote about their parents' jobs. Write the names of the places where some of the parents work. Remember to underline the titles of magazines, newspapers, and books.

Uptown Moving Vans

_____

- -

_____

Wildlife Magazine

_____

- -

_____

Ned's Animal Hospital

_____

- -

_____

Yvette's Kitchen

_____

- -

_____

Evaluation

Remember: All letters should rest on the bottom line.

Write the sentences.

Mayor Karl Utley works at City Hall.

_____

- -

_____

_____

- -

_____

Vicky Young reports for the <u>Weekly News</u>.

_____

- -

_____

_____

- -

_____

Check Your Handwriting

Do all your letters rest on the bottom line?

Yes ☐   No ☐

Writing Proper Nouns

Special names for people, places, and things are called proper nouns. Proper nouns begin with capital letters. Write these proper nouns.
Use cursive handwriting.

Miss Helen Ko

65 East Villa Avenue

Omaha, Nebraska

North America

Wednesday

November 21

Charlie Needs a Cloak

Writing Cursive T and F

Cursive **T** and **F** look a little like manuscript **T** and **F.** Trace and write the letters.

Trace and write the sentence. Do not join cursive **T** and **F** to the letters that follow them.

Fred will go to Tim's party on Friday.

Fred will go to Tim's party on Friday.

Writing Cursive B

Cursive **B** looks like manuscript **B.** Trace and write the letter.

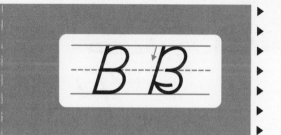

$\mathcal{B}\mathcal{B}$ $\mathcal{B}$ $\mathcal{B}$ $\mathcal{B}$

Trace and write the sentences. Do not join cursive **B** to the letter that follows it.

Birthdays are fun.

Birthdays are fun.

Becky gave Bonnie a birthday gift.

Becky gave Bonnie a birthday gift.

Writing Cursive P and R

You can see manuscript **P** and **R** in cursive **P** and **R**. Trace and write the letters.

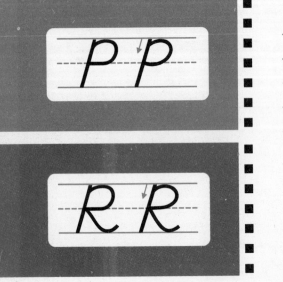

P P   *P   P*   *P*

R R   *R   R*   *R*

Trace and write the sentences.
Join cursive **R** to the letter that follows it.
Do not join cursive **P** to the next letter.

Paul opens the door.

Paul opens the door.

Please come in, Rita.

Please come in, Rita.

Writing an Invitation

Brian Riley is having a birthday party. He sent invitations to his friends.

Copy Brian's invitation. Write smaller than usual to fit the words on the lines. Try to make your tall letters twice as tall as your small letters.

You're Invited!

What: _a Birthday Party for Brian Riley_

When: _Friday, May 31_
_4:00 P.M._

Where: _32 Tower Trail_

Please Come!

You're Invited!

What: _____

_____

When: _____

_____

Where: _____

Please Come!

Practice

Write the letters.

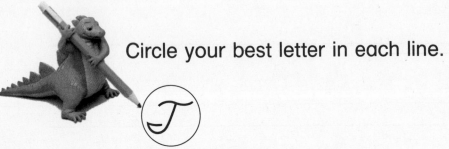

Circle your best letter in each line.

Write the date and the address.

Tuesday, February 5

78 Bent Pine Road

Review

Write the names of the children who came to Kim's birthday party.

Penny
_____
- - - - - - - - - - - - - - - - - - -
_____
_____

Robert
_____
- - - - - - - - - - - - - - - - - - -
_____

Felipe
_____
- - - - - - - - - - - - - - - - - - -
_____
_____

Tony
_____
- - - - - - - - - - - - - - - - - - -
_____

Rachel
_____
- - - - - - - - - - - - - - - - - - -
_____
_____

Fran
_____
- - - - - - - - - - - - - - - - - - -
_____

Brett
_____
- - - - - - - - - - - - - - - - - - -
_____

Paula
_____
- - - - - - - - - - - - - - - - - - -
_____

Evaluation

 **Remember:** Do not join capital **T, F, B,** or **P** to the next letter.

Write the sentences.

Today is Ramona Fox's birthday.

_____

- -

_____

_____

- -

_____

Put some cake on Ben's plate.

_____

- -

_____

_____

- -

_____

Check Your Handwriting
Did you remember not to join capital
T, F, B, or **P** to the next letter?

Yes No
☐   ☐

114

Writing Cursive G and S

Cursive **G** and **S** do not look like manuscript
G and **S**. Trace and write the letters.

G *G*   *G G G*   *G*

S *S*   *S S S*   *S*

Trace and write the sentence. Do
not join cursive **G** and **S** to the
letters that follow them.

Gabe Soto went to the Science Museum.

Gabe Soto went to the

Science Museum.

Writing Cursive I

Cursive **I** does not look like manuscript **I**. Trace and write the letter.

I I

I I . . I

Trace and write the sentences.
Join cursive **I** to the letter that follows it.
Always write the pronoun **I** with a capital letter.

Irene and I like the Insect Room.

Irene and I like the Insect Room.

Insects are interesting.

Insects are interesting.

Writing Cursive Q and Z

Cursive **Q** and **Z** do not look like manuscript **Q** and **Z**. Trace and write the letters.

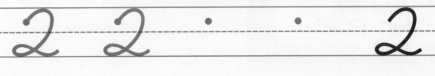

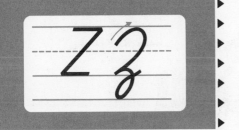

Trace and write the sentence. Join cursive **Q** and **Z** to the letters that follow them.

Zeb asked Mr. Quinn a question.

Zeb asked Mr. Quinn a question.

Writing Cursive D

Cursive **D** looks something like manuscript **D**.
Trace and write the letter.

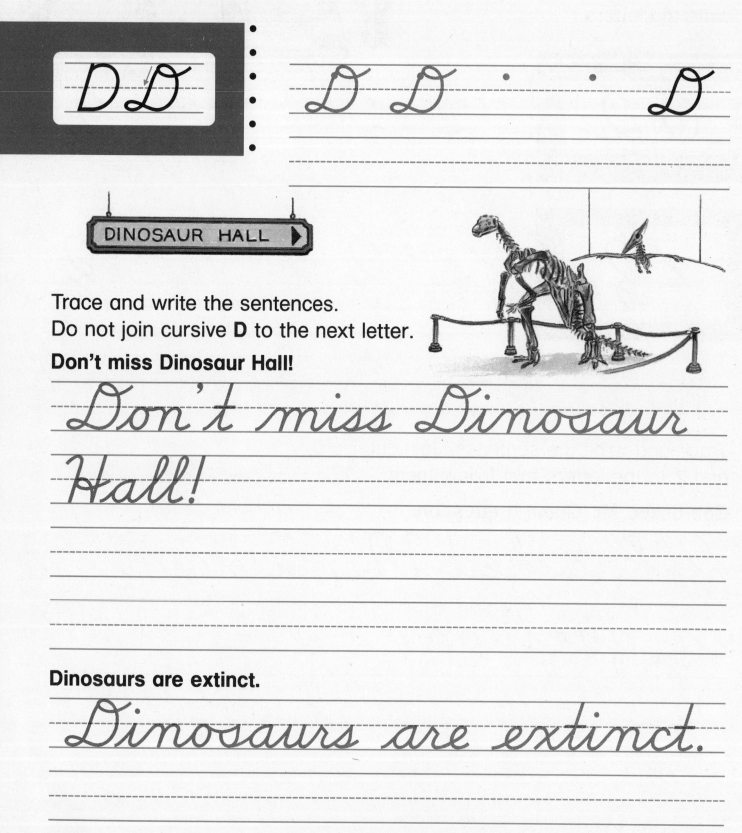

$\mathcal{D}\mathcal{D}$ $\mathcal{D}$ $\mathcal{D}$ $\cdot$ $\cdot$ $\mathcal{D}$

DINOSAUR HALL ▶

Trace and write the sentences.
Do not join cursive **D** to the next letter.

Don't miss Dinosaur Hall!

Don't miss Dinosaur Hall!

Dinosaurs are extinct.

Dinosaurs are extinct.

Writing Cursive J

Cursive **J** does not look like manuscript **J.** Trace and write the letter.

 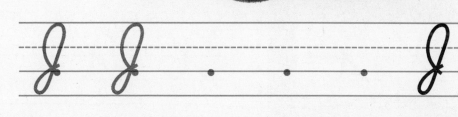

Trace and write the sentences. Join cursive **J** to the letter that follows it.

Josh and Jenny saw a model of Jupiter.

Josh and Jenny saw a model of Jupiter.

Just look at this, Joe!

Just look at this, Joe!

119

Writing Cursive X and L

You can see manuscript **X** in cursive **X**.
Cursive **L** looks something like manuscript **L**.
Trace and write the letters.

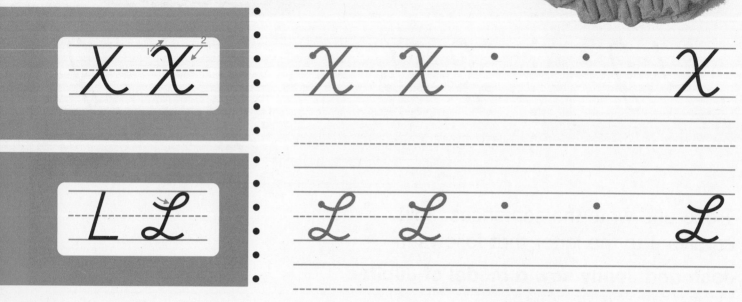

Trace and write the sentence.
Join cursive **L** to the letter that follows it.
Do not join cursive **X** to the next letter.

Look at the fossils in Room X.

Look at the fossils in
Room X.

Writing a Thank-you Note

Mrs. Green's class visited the Natural History Museum.
The children wrote a thank-you note to the museum guide.
Copy the note. Slant all your letters the same way.

March 7, 200_

Dear Ms. Jones,

Thank you for showing us around the museum. We all learned a lot.

Your friends,
Mrs. Green's class

Practice

Write the letters.

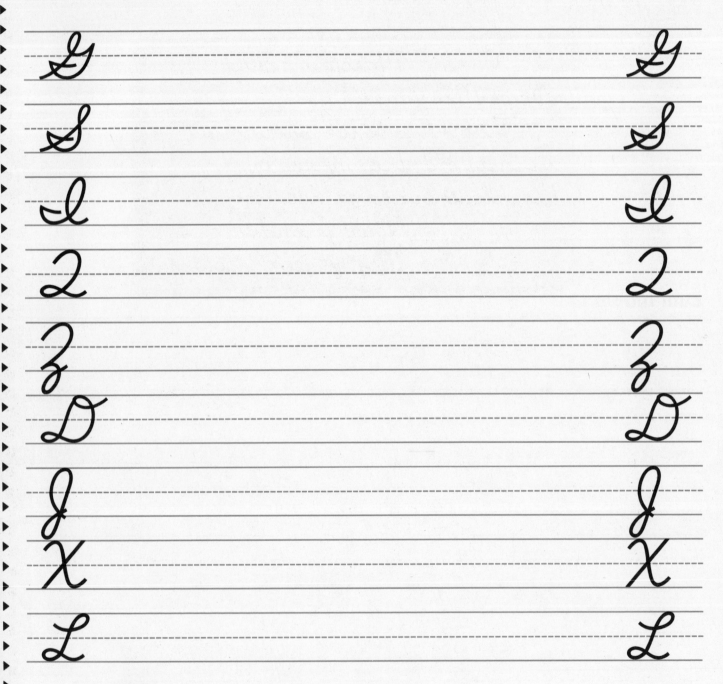

Circle your best letter in each line.

Review

Write the words on the museum signs. Use cursive.

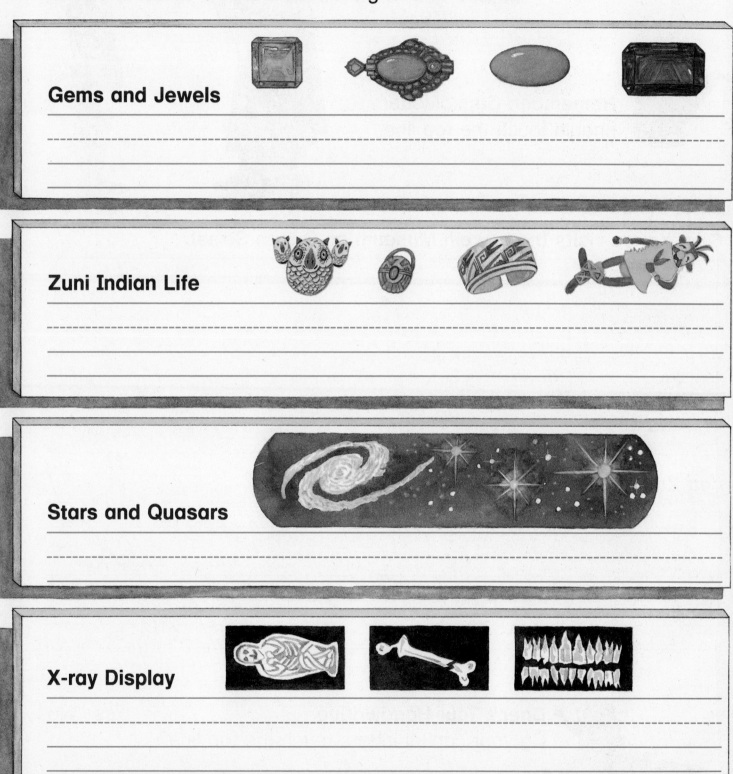

Gems and Jewels

Zuni Indian Life

Stars and Quasars

X-ray Display

Evaluation

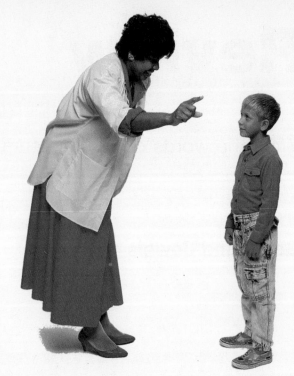

Remember: Capital letters should touch the top line.

Write the sentences.

Gina Xanos visits the Lincoln Museum on Queen Street.

_____

_____

_____

_____

_____

_____

Jeff Zale stops at the Information Desk.

_____

_____

_____

_____

_____

Check Your Handwriting
Do your capital letters touch the top line?

Yes No
☐   ☐

Reading and Writing

Gail Gibbons wrote a book about natural history museums. It's called *Dinosaurs, Dragonflies, and Diamonds: All About Natural History Museums.*

Read some sentences from her book that tell about activities that happen behind the scenes at a museum.

Scientists come to natural history museums to study the vast collections. Behind closed doors, they take their notes. They find drawers and drawers of stones . . . animal bones . . . Indian clothing . . . beetles. . . . Millions and millions of objects are stored here.

Behind the scenes, it takes many workers for the museums to run smoothly. Some workers are busy labeling, tagging, and recording all of the many stored items.

Staff scientists work in their labs, making new discoveries about nature and people.

Museums often create new exhibits, too. ■

If you could look behind the scenes at a museum, what things would you want to see? Make a list of them. Think about why you would like to see them.

_____

_____

_____

_____

_____

_____

_____

_____

John wishes he could see how a museum makes a new exhibit. He wrote this sentence to tell why.

I wonder howthey make plants,and animals look soreal.

Look at what John wrote.   Yes   No
- Did he tell why he would like to see how a new exhibit is made?   ☐   ☐

Look at how John wrote it.
- Are all his letters slanted the same way?   ☐   ☐
- Is there always enough space between his words?   ☐   ☐

Circle the letters that are not slanted the same way. Make an **X** between words that don't have enough space between them.

126

Choose the most interesting thing from the list you made on page 126. Write about it. Tell why you would like to see it.

_____
- -
_____
- -
_____
_____
- -
_____
_____
- -
_____
_____
- -
_____
_____
- -
_____

Look at what you wrote.   Yes   No
- Did you tell what you would like to see?   ☐   ☐
- Did you tell why you would like to see it?   ☐   ☐

Look at how you wrote it.
- Are all your letters slanted the same way?   ☐   ☐
- Is there enough space between your words?   ☐   ☐

Make any changes that are needed. Then make a clean copy on another sheet of paper.

Index

Abbreviations, 99
Adjusting handwriting
  size, 21, 92, 111
  without writing lines, 21, 99
Capitalization
  of addresses on envelopes, 99
  of pronoun *I*, 31, 116
  of proper nouns, 13, 96, 107, 112
  of sentences, 13
  of title, Mrs., 45
Common-stroke letter groups, cursive
  capitals
    A, C, E, O, 94–98
    H, K, N, M, U, V, W, Y, 100–106
    T, F, B, P, R, 108–110, 112–114
  lower-case
    l, h, k, t, i, u, e, j, p, 61–68
    a, d, c, n, m, x, g, y, q, 69–76
    o, w, b, 78–82
Common-stroke letter groups, manuscript
  aA, dD, oO, gG, cC, eE, sS, 12–20
  fF, bB, lL, tT, hH, kK, 22–28
  iI, uU, wW, yY, jJ, rR, nN, mM, pP, 30–40
  qQ, vV, zZ, xX, 42–45, 48–50
Cursive handwriting
  capitals, 94–98, 100–106, 108–110, 112–120, 122–124
  joining strokes, 41, 54, 88, 94–95, 100–103, 108–110, 115–120
    ending, 55, 56
    overhill, 56, 69, 70, 71, 72, 73, 78, 83
    sidestroke, 57, 78, 79, 80, 83, 87
    uphill, 55, 61, 62, 63, 64, 65, 78, 79, 84, 85, 86
  lower-case, 61–76, 78–86, 88–90
Directions, writing, 29
Envelope, addressing an, 99
Evaluating handwriting, 8, 9, 10, 18, 20, 26, 28, 38, 40, 48, 50, 52–53, 66, 68, 74, 76, 77, 80, 82, 88, 90, 91, 96, 98, 104, 106, 112, 114, 122, 124, 126–127. *See also* Legibility
Evaluation, 20, 28, 40, 50, 68, 76, 82, 90, 98, 106, 114, 124. *See also* Legibility
Everyday writing
  envelope, 99
  directions, 29
  invitation, 111
  labels, 21
  list, 92
  proper nouns, 107
  thank-you note, 121
I, **capitalization of,** 31, 116

Invitation, writing an, 111
Joining Strokes. *See* Cursive handwriting
Labels, writing, 21
Legibility
  letter form, 8, 60, 91, 99
  letter size, 8, 52–53, 60, 91, 111
  letter slant, 9, 77, 91, 121, 126–127
  letter spacing, 10, 29, 77, 91
  word spacing, 10, 29, 77, 91, 126–127
Letter form, 8, 60, 91, 99
Letters
  cursive capitals
    A, 94; B, 109; C, 94; D, 118; E, 95; F, 108; G, 115; H, 100; I, 116; J, 119; K, 100; L, 120; M, 101; N, 101; O, 95; P, 110; Q, 117; R, 110; S, 115; T, 108; U, 102; V, 102; W, 103; X, 120; Y, 103; Z, 117
  cursive lower-case
    a, 69; b, 79; c, 70; d, 70; e, 64; f, 86; g, 72; h, 61; i, 63; j, 65; k, 62; l, 61; m, 71; n, 71; o, 78; p, 65; q, 73; r, 85; s, 84; t, 62; u, 63; v, 83; w, 78; x, 72; y, 73; z, 83
  manuscript
    aA, 12–13; bB, 22–23; cC, 14–15; dD, 12–13; eE, 16–17; fF, 22–23; gG, 14–15; hH, 24–25; iI, 30–31; jJ, 34–35; kK, 24–25; lL, 22–23; mM, 36–37; nN, 36–37; oO, 12–13; pP, 36–37; qQ, 42–43; rR, 34–35; sS, 16–17; tT, 24–25; uU, 30–31; vV, 42–43; wW, 32–33; xX, 44–45; yY, 32–33; zZ, 44–45
Letter size, 8, 52–53, 60, 91, 111
Letter slant, 9, 77, 91, 121, 126–127
Letter spacing, 10, 29, 77, 91
List, writing a, 92
Numbers, 46–47, 48
Position for writing, 6–7
Practice, 18, 26, 38, 48, 66, 74, 80, 88, 96, 104, 112, 122
Proper nouns, writing, 13, 107
Punctuation marks
  apostrophe, 23
  comma, 25
  exclamation marks, 23
  period, 13, 45
  question mark, 13
  underlining titles, 105
Reading and writing, 51–53, 125–127
Review, 19, 27, 39, 49, 67, 75, 81, 89, 97, 105, 113, 123
Thank-you note, writing a, 121
Transition to cursive, 41, 54–58
Word spacing, 10, 29, 77, 91, 126–127
Writing. *See* Reading and writing